UNAPOLOGETICALLY FEMININE

Red Flags, French Men & Returning to Yourself

From Parisian Chaos to Feminine Essence—Dating, Healing, and Holding Your Standards High

LUCIA PETRUSOVA

Author's note.

This book is based on real events, real French men, and real WTF moments. If you recognize yourself in these pages.....well, maybe take that as a sign to work on your communication skills. Or your bank account. Or both.

Either way, thank you for the content.

Disclaimer:
No French men were harmed in the making of this book....but a few egos were bruised.

This book is a work of nonfiction based on personal experiences. Some names and identifying details have been changed to protect the privacy of individuals.

English version edited with the assistance of AI (ChatGPT), under the author's full creative direction.

Photos by: Iveta Ripert, Iveta Ripert Photography

Cover by: Lucia Petrusova, Veronika Ivanova Design Pixel Lab

For translation or media inquiries, please contact:
luciapetrusovatherapy@luciapetrusova.com
www.luciapetrusova.com

Published by Maison Lutencia

First Edition, 2025

Printed and distributed worldwide via online platforms

ISBN : 979-10-980941-0-1

This book is more than just a dating survival guide—it's a journey through the world of French men and the ultimate power of stepping into your feminine essence. A woman who knows her worth, sets her standards, and embodies both softness and unpredictability is truly magnetic. When a woman shifts her internal world, the external world has no choice but to follow.

ACKNOWLEDGMENTS

To the woman I've become.
To every version of me who lived through these pages.

INTRODUCTION

WHEN A WOMAN REMEMBERS WHO SHE IS

Let me tell you a secret: I didn't write this book because I've figured it all out.

I wrote this book because I was tired of playing roles that were never mine to begin with. Tired of pretending to be the "cool woman" who doesn't need much. The "understanding woman" who adjusts, accommodates, and smiles politely while her needs quietly starve.

I wrote this book after realizing that the men I was attracting weren't random—they were mirrors. Some were beautifully wrapped illusions. Others were walking red flags I tried to paint white. But all of them—every single one—were invitations. Not to love harder. But to love myself deeper.

And maybe, as you turn these pages, you'll recognize one of your own chapters too.

Because the truth is: relationships are never just about the other person. They're about us. They reveal what's unresolved, what's unhealed, and what we still believe we're worthy of.

And for many women—especially high-achieving, independent, capable women—there's a dangerous blind spot. We think we've done "the work." But we're still accepting crumbs and calling it connection. Still confusing chemistry with compatibility. Still shrinking ourselves to fit into someone else's bandwidth.

Why?

Because no one ever taught us how to set the bar.

In a world where women are constantly told to soften, to be less intimidating, to be more patient, to be "understanding" of his career, his divorce, his healing journey, his everything—we forgot something vital:

That our needs matter.
That our standards are sacred.

And that it is not our job to be chosen. It is our job to choose ourselves so fully that we only attract those who are able and willing to meet us there.

That's why I wrote this book.

Not to give you another checklist of red flags (although, trust me, there are plenty in here). But to invite you into your sovereignty. To remind you that you are not "too much." You're just too powerful to keep shrinking. Too radiant to keep waiting. Too alive to keep performing for love that doesn't know how to hold you.

This book is part memoir, part mirror. It's a collection of stories—some tragic, some hilarious—about the men I dated, the illusions I bought into, and the woman I finally became when I stopped outsourcing my worth to unavailable men in expensive shoes.

It's about standards.
Not the superficial kind—
But the energetic kind.

The kind etched into your nervous system after one too many "almosts." The kind that don't just protect you—but magnetize what you truly desire.

And here's the wild part: the moment I healed the unresolved, the moment I recalibrated my energy, everything changed.

My relationships.
My business.
My body.
My frequency.

Because when a woman stops accepting breadcrumbs, the universe stops sending her beggars.

When a woman reclaims her power, her energy becomes selective.
She no longer chases. She magnetizes.
She no longer performs. She embodies.
She no longer waits for love. She becomes it.

Maybe you've felt it too—that strange ache, that quiet grief, the sense that you don't belong anywhere. That no one sees you beneath the mask.

I know that feeling.
I lived there for a while.

But this book is your exit route.
Not into a fantasy.
But into truth.
Into sovereignty.
Into love that doesn't require your self-abandonment.

So if you've ever wondered:

> Why do I attract men who aren't ready?
> Why do I feel so powerful in business but so powerless in love?

> Why do I stay in things that don't make me feel seen?

Then this book is for you.

It's for the women who are done lowering their frequency to make someone else feel safe.
It's for the women who are ready to stop earning love—and start allowing it.

It's for the woman who knows—deep down—that her story isn't over.
That her softness isn't weakness.
That her standards are not a wall, but a doorway.
And that her real love story starts when she refuses to disappear ever again.

This is not just about men.
This is about you.
And your sovereign return.

Welcome to the pages where you finally become unforgettable—
To them, maybe.
But more importantly…
To yourself.

CONTENTS

PART 1

DATING STORIES – THE CHAOS BEFORE THE CLARITY

Before I reclaimed my standards, my worth, and my feminine power… I dated.

And not just any men—French men. Narcissists, ghosters, gamblers, charmers, emotionally unavailable geniuses, and even a catfish with Google-searchable lies. Each chapter in this part is a story—sometimes hilarious, sometimes heartbreaking—but all of them led me back to myself.

This is where the breadcrumbs were served, the patterns repeated, and the illusions lived large. I wrote them all down not to shame anyone, but to reflect the ways so many of us abandon ourselves in the name of "love." These pages are a mirror. You might laugh. You might cringe. You might recognize yourself.

This is the chaos before the clarity. The fire before the phoenix. The part where the feminine still tries to earn what was never hers to chase.

Welcome to Part One.

CHAPTER

1

THE ART OF BEING STINGY

Let me start with a fundamental fact you must know: I have always been a financially independent woman. No exceptions. No apologies.

And yet, somehow, I ended up with a man who made Scrooge look like a generous philanthropist.

It all began with my very first French date. Love at first sight? No. In fact, I didn't even like him. He was not my style at all. I don't even know why I said yes to the date—maybe the constellations were strange that day.

He took me to a restaurant for dinner, and the conversation was as dry as a baguette left out in the sun for a week. I thought, *Okay, maybe he's just nervous.*

Second date? A walk, then lunch. Still boring. But hey, who knows—maybe he's a slow burner.

Apparently, he didn't think so. Because he was obsessed with me.

After our dates, he called me **every. single. day.** I kept wondering: *How is it possible that someone with the personality of a boiled potato in person can turn into a full-blown radio host over the phone?* A mystery.

Somehow, we ended up dating for years. He took me on vacations. He paid for everything. He was attentive, caring. It was all great.

Until we moved in together.

That's when the Stinginess Olympics began. Everything became 50/50. Groceries. Vacations. Even a mysterious "shared expenses contribution" he invented—amount unclear, purpose even more unclear—despite the fact that we lived in *his* house, not mine.

Yes, even vacations.
One day, I woke up and thought: *Am I in a trap?*
The answer was a screaming **HELL YES.**

This man had been running a long-term financial illusion. He was the God of Generosity—pulling off the greatest disappearing act of all time.

But the real climax?
The moment I dared to buy something nice for myself.

I had worked hard, earned a bonus, and decided to treat myself to a **Classic Caviar Leather Chanel bag**. A masterpiece. A symbol of success. A well-deserved reward.

And then… the meltdown.

He. Lost. His. Mind.

A full-blown performance about how I was irresponsible, how I should have spent that money on a vacation together instead of a "stupid bag."

The best part? He gave me the silent treatment for a week.

Oh honey, you think you're punishing me?
I had never enjoyed peace and quiet so much in my life.

But unlike him, I play smart.

While he was sulking over my handbag, I was preparing my exit strategy. Because let me tell you something: **when a man suddenly changes the moment you live together or marry him, he hasn't changed—he just stopped pretending.**

The final cherry on top?
When I told him it was over, he looked at me, dead serious, and asked:

"But… where will you go? Where will you live?"

Ah, *mon chéri*… I had a life before you.
And unlike you, I don't need a sugar mommy to survive.

Oh, and about the ring…

Before we moved in together, he did something very romantic. He bought me a diamond ring.
Well… a "diamond" ring. At least, that's what he claimed.

It wasn't anything extravagant, but according to him, a diamond was there.

Fast forward to post-breakup, and let me be clear: I wasn't about to return that ring. Nope. I was going to do something much better.

Sell it.

I walked into the jeweler's feeling like a queen—ready to cash in on a tiny slice of emotional damages. The lady behind the counter examined the ring with her little magnifying glass, nodded politely, and then…

The humiliation of my life began.

> "Madame… this is… steel."

I blinked.
Pardon?

> "Yes, steel. And this stone… um… let's just say, no one in their right mind puts a real diamond into *steel*."

Ah.
C'est fantastique.

And that's how I left the shop with my steel masterpiece still in hand, my dignity shattered into a million pieces, and my last drop of faith in men evaporating into thin air.

LESSONS LEARNED:

Rule #1: A woman must always be financially independent.
Money = Power.
Money = Freedom.
Money = Voice.
Never forget it.

Rule #2: Before you commit, investigate his family history.
Was his mother financially dependent on his father?

Did his father control the money?
Spoiler alert: If he grew up thinking women should just "contribute emotionally" while men hold the financial power—run.

Rule #3: Pay attention to how he reacts when you spend money on yourself.
Does he get offended?
Does he make snide comments?
That's a sign.

BONUS: Questions to Ask on a First Date to Detect a Future Stingy King

- "What's your opinion on splitting bills in a relationship?"
  (If he says *'It should always be 50/50 no matter what'*—alert mode ON.)

- "Do you like eating out? How do you choose restaurants?"
  (If he says *'I always find a great restaurant with a great discount'*—girl, run.)

- "What do you think about luxury handbags?"
  (If he rolls his eyes—abort the mission immediately.)

- "How do you feel about financially supporting a partner?"

(If he laughs uncomfortably—prepare for your future as a co-signer on every bill.)

- "What's the most expensive thing you've ever bought for yourself?"
  (If he proudly says *'A Rolex imitation made in China but looks authentic'*—girl, run and never look back.)

CHAPTER

2

Monsieur Mystère: The Diamond Mirage

Well, well… enter Monsieur Mystère.

He appeared just three months after I escaped from Stingy King. And let me tell you—from day one, the love bombing was **INTENSE**.

We're talking grand gestures, poetic compliments, deep eye contact as if he could see into my soul. It was like I'd walked straight into a fairy tale—except I forgot to check if it was written by the Grimm Brothers… or Stephen King.

Three weeks in, we were sitting in *Cartier*.

Yes, *Cartier*.

Guess why?

Because he wanted to buy me a diamond ring. A real one this time.
€37,000 worth of diamond.

Now, let me tell you—my brain was still healthy at this point. Not yet manipulated. And something inside me went:

"Wait a minute… wasn't I just dating a guy who almost had a heart attack over a Chanel bag? And now this one wants to drop 37K on a ring he hasn't even seen on my finger yet?"

But oh, the love bombing continued.

I was living my best Parisian dream—Michelin-starred restaurants, exclusive nightclubs, romantic château weekends. I felt like I had finally entered the life I deserved.

But the ring?

It was never purchased.

And do you know why?

Because, *mon amour*, **Monsieur Mystère was broke**. Completely. Utterly. Tragically.

But Then, the Cracks Appeared

He started blaming his ex-wife for never buying him a single gift. He blamed the couple's therapist for being incompetent. He blamed the world for his inability to connect.

Poor him. Always the misunderstood one. Always the giver who never got anything back.

And I started realizing—this wasn't emotional intelligence.
This was polished narcissism in a cashmere sweater.

He was never at fault. Ever. His stories were always crafted to trigger guilt, sympathy, and admiration.

The more I listened, the more I heard the pattern:

> *"I'm the good guy. It's the women who don't get me."*

What I thought was depth was deflection.
What I mistook for confidence was actually **chronic avoidance**, dressed as charm.

And then it hit me—quietly, but clearly:

> He's not looking for connection.
> He's looking for **control**—emotional, energetic, sexual.

And I? I had flipped the script.
Now, he didn't know how to play me.

The moment I stopped chasing—he froze.
The moment I pulled back—he had no tools to meet me.

Because he wasn't built for real intimacy.
He was built for **transactions**.

And I?
I don't sell. I don't discount. I don't perform.

While I was living the illusion of romance, he was living his best life elsewhere.

Because as we know, **narcissists always have a backup plan**—a side project, and a little secret hobby called "managing multiple women at the same time."

Now, you might ask:

"Lucia, how did you even attract this guy?"

The answer is simple.

I was simply unhappy with Stingy King.
With him, everything was transactional. I had no social life. No nightlife.
I was just a walking **TARGET**. That's it.

And Monsieur Mystère? Oh, he knew.

They always know.

Narcissists have a built-in radar for vulnerable people. They can sense when you're lacking something—love, attention, affection, excitement, emotional depth—and they give you **ALL of it at once**.

Until, of course, they take it all away.

The 30-Day Rule

Now, here's something crucial:
Our brain has exactly **30 days** to recognize manipulation.

That's how long it takes before those little red flags start making sense.

But do you think it's easy?
No. Because love bombing hacks the system.

Your brain gets addicted. The ups, the downs, the "I love you" followed by the silent treatment. The manipulation. The guilt-tripping. The moments of pure bliss, mixed with emotional withdrawal. It's a rollercoaster.

And before you know it, you're **hooked**.

Let me tell you—**withdrawal from a narcissist is worse than giving up sugar, caffeine, alcohol, and hard drugs at the same time.**

So Here's What I Learned:

- If it feels too good to be true in the first month?
  It is.
- If he makes you feel like the most special woman alive, but your gut says *"Hmm... something's off"*—**listen to your gut.**
- If he offers you a diamond ring in week three, **make sure he can afford lunch first.**
- If he calls his ex *"crazy"*—**honey, you're next.**
- If he disappears for hours, he's not *"busy"*—he's **BUSY.**

  According to **Criminal Behavior Analyst Laura Richards**, in one of her podcast interviews, women should never overshare on a first date about their past relationships or describe in detail the type of man they're looking for. Oversharing gives narcissists and psychopaths a free blueprint—they adapt to hook you in.

And most importantly:

If your brain ever whispers:

"Run, Lucia, run..."
Don't ask questions.
Just grab your Chanel bag—and **GO.**

Why We Fall for Narcissists:

The Chemistry Trap & The Mirror Game

The attraction wasn't a mistake. It was **chemical. Biological. Familiar.**

And for many of us, that kind of magnetic pull is often misunderstood as destiny.

It's not.

It's the body responding to a **subconscious pattern**—one that was likely wired long before we ever matched with a narcissist.

Here's what nobody tells you:

> The chemistry you feel with a narcissist **isn't love**—it's a **survival memory.**

The tension. The unpredictability. The charm. The thrill of being seen—
And then suddenly... not.

For women who grew up feeling emotionally unsafe, unseen, or who had to **perform** to receive love—this dynamic feels oddly like home.

But it's not safe.
It's **nervous system activation.**

The highs are euphoric.
The lows are confusing.
The craving is real.

Because your body is trying to **complete the loop** it never finished as a little girl:

> *"If I can just be good enough... sexy enough... smart enough... maybe this time, I'll be chosen."*

CHAPTER

3

JACKPOT OR JACKASS? THE GAMBLER WHO BET ON MY WALLET

There's something you should know about me.

I was raised by a detective.

Well, not exactly.
My grandfather was an inspector in the police force—always on the front line, chasing down criminals, gun in hand.

And I?

I inherited his brain.

As a child, I spent my days soaking in his stories, hanging on every thrilling detail of his chases, arrests, and interrogations. My grandmother was the softer one—full of love and warmth—but my grandfather? He was my hero.

So naturally, I grew up suspicious.
Of everything.

And when it came to dating, let's just say—every man was guilty until proven innocent.

Which brings me to **Monsieur Jackass**.

Oh, this one was special.

From the moment we met, my internal sirens were blaring.

On the first date, he proudly declared that he had won **a million euros in poker**.

Oh? Fascinating. Tell me more.

He continued—he was one of the best players in the game, practically a legend.

Oh? Intriguing. Go on.

He had strategy, skill, and intuition.

Impressive. I leaned in, pretending to be captivated.

Because this had potential—not as a love story, but as a **premium chapter in my book**.

Naturally, I agreed to a second date.
Not because I was interested.
But because I was waiting for the moment he would inevitably reveal himself as a fraud.

And oh—he did **not** disappoint.

Somewhere between the cheap wine and his bragging about VIP casino lounges, he casually dropped a brilliant proposition:

> "You should invest in me."

Excuse me?

Yes, you heard that right.

He suggested I give him **€400** to play poker because he was so good, we were *guaranteed* to win.

Oh, darling.
The desperation. The confidence. The sheer **audacity**.

He really thought I was dumb enough to fall for his self-proclaimed millionaire story—**after one date**?

Absolutely not.

I stared at him for a moment, wondering if he genuinely believed his own nonsense.

And then, with the sweetest smile, I leaned in and whispered:

> "How about this? *You* put in your million, and when *we* win, you can give me my cut."

Silence.

You see, the thing about addicts is that they always believe they're one game away from their big break.

This one?
He was already broke.
A **jackpot turned jackass**.

I paid for my own drink, stood up, and left.

Because I don't gamble.
Not with my money.
And definitely not with my time.

The Addict's Mind

Gambling, Desperation, and the Illusion of Control

Here's the thing about addiction—it's never really about the thing itself.

Gambling. Alcohol. Drugs. Love. Work. Even relationships.
Addiction is a symptom, not the disease.

At its core, addiction is about **escape**.
It's about filling a void.
Numbing discomfort.
Chasing a fleeting high.
Grasping at an illusion of control.

And gambling? Oh, it's a **masterpiece of self-destruction** wrapped in a fantasy of intelligence.

The gambler believes he has a system.
He believes he can't lose—that with just one more bet, one more game, one more night at the table, his luck will change.

But it never does.

And even if it *does* for a moment, the win is never enough.

The thrill isn't in **having** money—it's in **risking** it.

The illusion of power. The adrenaline rush. The fantasy of outsmarting the game.
That is the addiction.

And it doesn't stop with poker chips and roulette wheels.

Some people gamble with **love.**
Some gamble with **trust.**
Some gamble with their **entire future**, believing they can fix their problems if they just play one more round.

Addicts don't think rationally.
They justify.
They chase.
They drag you down with them—if you let them.

And the worst part?

They **believe their own lies.**

So when Monsieur Jackass looked me in the eye and suggested I "invest" in him, he wasn't just trying to scam me—
He was **scamming himself.**

And that, ladies, is why you never, ever fund a man's addiction.

Not with your money.
Not with your time.
And definitely not with your **heart**.

CHAPTER

4

VOULEZ-VOUS PAYER AVEC MOI CE SOIR?

This one? One date. And the last.
But at least I taught him a lesson.

On Tinder, he looked promising—an entrepreneur, into surfing and yoga. His profile screamed worldly, active, and successful. Add to that a good-looking face, and I thought, *Why not?*

It was a warm summer evening, and he took me to a terrace for a glass of wine. Just wine. But that's the beauty of France—it doesn't matter where you go, the wine is always great.
(*The coffee? A different story.*)

We talked for about 40 minutes—nice conversation, nothing groundbreaking. Then, he suggested a walk.

Why not, right? We were near the Eiffel Tower. It sounded like a lovely idea.

And that's when the disaster happened.

He stood up, walked to the bar, and asked for the bill.
A grand total of **10 euros**.

Then—and this is where it gets good—he turned to me and waved me over.
Like a restaurant manager calling a waiter.

I walked up, a bit confused. And then came the masterpiece:

> "You can pay for your glass."

Oh.
Ohhh.

I swiped my card (of course I can afford my wine—that's not the point). Then I turned to him and gave him a lesson **his mother should've given him.**

> "This is cheap. I have never had a man—especially on a first date—ask me to pay for my own drink in such a tacky way.
> A man should be doing everything to impress me, not giving me 'pay for your wine' hand gestures."

And believe me, I was **impressed**.

I continued—giving him a monologue so powerful, it could have been a **TED Talk on dating standards**.

> "I don't need a man to pay my bills.
> But I want a man who can *afford a woman.*
> And darling, I am way out of your league."

The truth? He was broke.
A broke "entrepreneur," scamming his way through dating apps—probably hoping to find a naive woman who would split the check, or better yet, pick up the whole thing.

The next day, he messaged me.

He apologized, saying he wasn't ready for a relationship.
(Lol. No kidding.)

Then came the best part:

> He asked if we could **stay friends**.

Yeah.
No.

Why Women Should NEVER Accept 50/50 in Dating

Ladies, let's talk about this "modern equality" nonsense in dating.

Dating is **not** a roommate agreement.

If a man insists on splitting every bill from the start, he's setting the tone for a **transactional** relationship.
Not romance.
Not care.
Just… math.

Men invest in what they value.
Look around—men have no issue spending money on expensive watches, tech, cars.
So if he hesitates to invest in you… what does that tell you?

Biology is real.
Whether people like it or not, men and women have different roles in dating.

Men are wired to pursue and provide—not because women *can't* afford things, but because this is **how attraction works**.

A man who is stingy with money is **stingy with love**.

Let's be real—if a guy is cheap in the beginning, it only gets worse.
The man who can't cover a €10 bill without blinking will absolutely have problems providing in a relationship—**emotionally and financially**.

Men know how to treat a woman **when they want to**.

If he's paying 50/50 with you, but paying for everything for someone else, that's a sign.

The right man won't even let you pull out your card—not because you can't, but because **he wants to**.

This isn't about gold-digging.

It's about choosing a partner who is **generous**, **stable**, and who **values you**.

Because if he can't cover a €5 glass of wine without making a scene...

> **What will happen when life actually gets hard?**

Exactly.

CHAPTER

5

FROM CELEBRITY TO CATFISH – HOW GOOGLE EXPOSED MY AFRICAN ROMEO

This one? Oh, he was special.

It all started when he slid into my DMs.
Smooth, charming—a classic social media flirt.

He told me he lived in Marseille and commented on one of my Instagram stories. Then he asked for the name of the restaurant I was at, claiming he was planning a trip to Paris and would love to check it out.

And just like that, the game began.

But before agreeing to meet a complete stranger, I insisted on a phone call.

Oh, did I mention? He was an *entrepreneur in real estate.*
(Ah yes—the universal scammer job title. Almost as popular as crypto traders and "import-export" business owners.)

The phone call was… suspicious.

The connection was horrible.

> "Where are you?" I asked. "Your signal is really bad."

He replied:

> "I'm in a very old building in Marseille… and there's a storm."

Mmm-hmm.

So I checked the weather.
Guess what? **No storm in Marseille.**

Busted.

And just like that, this went from a casual flirtation to a new chapter in my book.

I decided to play along.

I asked for a picture of him. Of course, he sent it—fast. Keep texting. Keeping things hot.

Meanwhile, I dragged his photo into **Google Reverse Image Search**.

And **BOOM**.

A scammer.
Pretending to be an American actor.

I laughed. **Hard.**

But I didn't stop there.
I kept playing.

For a whole month, I let him believe I was hooked.
And then… I started to sense something strange.

He was falling for me.

(Ah, the irony. The hunter became the hunted.)

Then Came the Plot Twist

One day, he messaged me:
He had to go to Africa to visit his *rich father*.

Oh, *go on*. I was dying to see where this would lead.

And it went there.

A few days later, he sent me a photo from a **hospital bed**.

He had been *attacked in the street*!
Violently robbed!
No money! No passport!

I laughed so hard, I almost fell off my chair.

Because…

> He sent me the **exact same photo** the American actor had posted on Instagram a year ago.

And then, the moment I had been waiting for—

> The **money request**.
>
> "Baby, please, I need your help. I was robbed, and now I have no way home. Could you send me just 600 euros?"

Oh, honey.

You are talking to the **wrong woman**.

I dropped the truth on him:

I knew everything.
He wasn't in Marseille.
He wasn't a real estate businessman.
He wasn't even 30.

And then came the biggest twist yet:

He confessed.

He told me he was actually **17 years old** and doing this because he needed money to study **coding**.

I couldn't even be mad.

The poor boy had **scammed himself.**
Fell into his own trap.

And believe it or not—he even sent me a real picture of himself.

At that point, I gave him a lecture **his mother should've given him**.

I told him to use his intelligence for something real. That he should actually **learn to code** instead of scamming women online.

And then, of course—
I blocked him.

How to Spot a Scammer Online

(AKA: Red Flags Wrapped in DMs)

Too Good to Be True

If they look like a model or celebrity but have 150 followers and no real-life photos—run.

Bad Connection?

Scammers always claim they have "bad service" or live in an "old building."
(*Translation: They're calling from a scam center in another country.*)

Over-the-Top Romance

If someone is professing their love too fast, they don't love *you*—they love your **bank account**.

They Can't Video Call

There's always an excuse. They're "shy," they're "busy," or—like this one—they're literally not the person in the pictures.

Sudden Tragic Events

They were robbed. They're in the hospital. Their father had a heart attack. (*And now they need your money.*)

Google Reverse Image Search Is Your Best Friend

If their photos are stolen, you'll find them. And when you do? Screenshot. Report. Block.

Never, Ever Send Money

If they ask you to send money, even once—**block, report, and move on.**

CHAPTER

6

THE MAN WHO ALMOST LOVED ME (BUT LOVED HIS EMOTIONAL BAGGAGE MORE)

We met two days before the second lockdown in Paris.
And let me tell you—it was the **Big Bang**.
A real crash. Instant attraction. Fireworks. Everything.

Until, of course, I realized he was emotionally unavailable.

And not just casually unavailable—
I mean *textbook-level* unavailable.
He had **all the symptoms**.

Smart. Handsome. Generous.

He loved great restaurants, wine, travel, and social life.
Basically, he loved everything… **except me**.

And yet, we were back and forth for almost **four years**.

Hilarious, right?

What I Know About Monsieur Baggage

Something bad happened to him. Either in childhood or in a past relationship.

His walls? Sky-high.
His heart? Locked.
And there wasn't a single window to slip through.

Signs of Emotional Unavailability?

Oh, he had them ALL:

- Hot and cold behavior (one day obsessed, the next day distant)
- Fear of commitment (*but also* fear of losing me)
- Avoidance of deep emotional conversations
- Prioritizing everything else over the relationship
- Keeping me close—but never too close

- Disappearing when things got real
- And the cherry on top? **Still active on dating apps while seeing me**

Yes, ladies and gentlemen.
He matched with **my friend**.

And not just that—he started a **conversation**.

Of course, she sent me everything.
And like the excellent best friend she is, she played her part well—according to my precise instructions.

When I confronted him, he did exactly what an emotionally unavailable man would do:
He disappeared.

Silence.
A whole **year** of silence.

Then—Plot Twist

He fell in love.
With **me**.

Oh, I felt it.

The sudden texts. The lingering messages.
The way his words started to sound like **regret**.

He was in his own trap now.

Watching me on social media.
Trying to guess if I was single.

(Yes. This is what men do.)

After a year, I finally replied.

And guess what?

He confessed everything.

He told me he had tried to forget me.
That he should've been an adult and told me he **loved me**.

Oh, NOW we're talking.

He took me to dinner.
We spent time together again.

And then—after two weeks of dating—he dropped the bomb:

> "I'm not sure I want to be in a relationship."

Let me decode that for you:

> "I don't want to be in a relationship... **with you**."

But somehow, we kept seeing each other for two more weeks.

And Here's Where It Gets Good

My libido?
Completely turned off.

Ladies, you know this superpower we have?
The one where, when a man treats us poorly, our body just **shuts down**?

Yeah. That happened.

I felt nothing.

Why?

Because my body knew—**before I did**—that this was over.

Meanwhile, his mid-life crisis was in full swing.
His testosterone levels weren't what they used to be.
(*A delicate topic for men, I know.*)

And let's be honest—there's help for that.

But him?

He didn't need **help**.
He needed **therapy**, **closure**, and a **reality check**.

And me?

I needed a man who actually knew what he wanted.

So I Walked Away

No regret.
No second-guessing.
Just a feeling of **relief**.

Because let's face it:

He wasn't my person.

He was just my **lesson**.

CHAPTER

7

GAME OVER: THE GENIUS, THE MESS, AND THE NO SHOW IN CANNES

We met on a dating app.
Great connection.
Brilliant intellectual conversations.
It all seemed promising.

Well—except for one small thing:

> **Two months in, and he still hadn't invited me to his place.**

Now, call me old-fashioned, but if a man avoids letting you see where he lives…
Something is up.

So, I did what any rational woman would do:
I **invited myself over**.

No, I didn't show up unannounced—I'm classy.
We actually agreed to spend the weekend at his house.

I arrived. I stayed two days.

The moment I stepped inside, I understood **why** he had kept it a secret:

> **Mess.**
> Absolute disaster.

Dark furniture covered in a 2cm-thick layer of dust—like a failed attempt at a Christmas village.

The dining table?
A chaotic battlefield of LEGO figures and children's toys.
I couldn't even find space to put down my glass of water.

> "Oh, your kids are here?" I asked, hoping this mess had an explanation.
>
> "No," he said.

Ah.
So this was just a **permanent museum exhibit**.

The Bedroom? Even Worse.

Forget anything remotely romantic.
It looked like a home office that had been hit by a tornado.

Papers. Wires. Books.
And God knows what else.

Honestly, I wasn't sure if I was supposed to sleep there…
or start filing tax returns.

"What's going on here?" I asked.

Excuses.
Excuses.
More excuses.

I told him I didn't feel well in his place (because, honestly, even my immune system was protesting and my libido had turned off forever) and suggested moving to a hotel.

He refused.

That's when I knew:

Game. Over.

So I left.

Then the Real Dots Started Connecting

He was **addicted to playing games on his phone**.
I mean, full-blown addiction.

Waking up in the middle of the night **just to play**.

Instead of trying to fall back asleep like a normal person,
he'd level up in whatever fantasy world he was living in.

And the mess?

Oh, that was just another symptom—of **depression**.

Now, I'm a hypnotherapist.
I could see the pattern.

But let's be clear:
I don't date clients.

He needed help—but **not from me**.

My job as a partner is to create a **supportive environment**,
not to drag a man to therapy while he finds endless excuses to avoid it.

We Broke Up.

But because life loves a plot twist,
he kept pursuing me—**inconsistently**, of course
(because that's also a symptom of depression).

He was sending me flowers.
Inconsistently too.

And one day, out of nowhere,
he planned a dreamy, romantic getaway in **Cannes**.

Beautiful hotel.
Stunning itinerary.

I arrived first.

He **never showed up**.

His excuse?

> "I couldn't get on the train."

Excuse me, what?

What are we talking about here—an existential crisis at the **SNCF station**?

He physically *could not enter* the train.

For a moment, I felt like **Carrie Bradshaw on her wedding day**.

Then reality hit me:

He had a **girlfriend** the whole time.

Ah.
So **French**!

My Response?

Let's just say I left him some very **expressive voice messages** to release my anger.

My last one?

A simple list of all my travel expenses…
And my bank account details.

Did He Ever Pay Me Back?

Yes.

But in the end, he did serve a purpose.

Because ironically, he was the one who always encouraged me to write this book.

So here you go, **Genius**.
Enjoy your chapter.

The Final Truth?

This man was fully supportive of my business—which was great.
He often told me he admired me.

But ladies… we don't need to be **admired** by men.

We need to be **desired**.

And me?

I need to feel admiration for **him**.
Otherwise… where is the attraction?

Moral of the Story?

If a man can't invite you over after two months, just assume:

- His living conditions are unfit for human life
  or
- He lives with other people

Either way?

Game over.

CHAPTER

8

THE PYRENEES PRINCE (WHO NEEDED A RICH MOMMY AND FREE MAID)

Ah, the Pyrenees Prince. Let's call him the Pyrénées Prince — because, well, he lived in the Pyrénées and acted like royalty, minus the throne… or income.

He had carefully curated the image of a worldly, sophisticated, emotionally deep, and accomplished man.

Total. Fake.

But let's give him credit—he had **charm**.
The kind that could almost make you overlook the obvious red flags.

On our very first date, he asked the waiter to take a photo of us and announced:

"This is a memory for our wedding one day."

... Excuse me, what?

I mean, **cute**—if I had actually agreed to marry him. Minor detail: he forgot to ask if I even *wanted* him in the first place.

Or maybe he thought I was a 44-year-old woman desperate to settle down.
No baby—
I am **not** desperate to marry **whomever**,
And **absolutely not** *you*.

Still, I let him entertain me.
After all, I'm a successful businesswoman.
He would *surely* do anything to impress me.

Until I found out that his bank account was **emptier than his promises**.

Now *that* was impressive.

At this point, I wasn't dating—I was collecting **material for my future book**.

Mommy Knows Best (And Pays for Everything)

This man was **completely dependent** on his mother.

And before you say, *"Oh, but that's sweet!"*—no, it was **not**.

His mother, by the way, was an **amazing woman**.
But here's the problem:

He took both of us to a restaurant.
Nice, right?

And then?

He let his **mother pay**.

I was shocked.

When I kindly pointed out that maybe, *just maybe*, a grown man should at least **pretend** to pick up the bill, his response?

"It's fine. Mum is full of money."

Well, well…
If he treats his mother like an ATM, I can only imagine what he expects from his girlfriend.

And I didn't have to imagine for long.

The Begging Begins

It started with small hints.

He wanted to sign up for an online self-development course.

Nice, right?
Self-growth. Very admirable.

Except—he had **no money** to subscribe.

So what did he say?

> "If you had money and were generous, you could subscribe for me."

… Oh, could I?

Let's see how far this will go.

A month into dating, he proposed we **move in together**.

… Sorry, what?

Was this a joke?

No, no. Pyrenees Prince was dead serious.

Narcissists love to **rush things**—it's their way of locking you in before you start seeing the cracks.

But me?
I had time.

So instead of moving in, I decided to spend a few weeks with him in his countryside house.

Correction: **his mother's** countryside house.

You know, like a scientist studying an exotic species in its natural habitat.

And let me tell you—I was **NOT** disappointed.

The Free Maid Experiment

Then—plot twist:
I got **Covid**.

I was sick.
Weak.
Trapped with him in one place.

Thank God we hadn't moved in together.

Here's where it gets good:

I was barely functioning.
He wasn't cooking.

Which wouldn't be a problem—we're in France, there's takeaway everywhere.

But that wasn't his strategy.

No, no.

His **master plan** was to wait for his **mother** to come to the house, do the grocery shopping, and cook for us.

See the pattern?

Meanwhile, I was starving, exhausted, and slowly turning into a skeleton.
I lost **five kilos** in two weeks.

But wait—it gets better.

Short-term rental & the Dying Housekeeper

Not only was he personally broke—
He was also broke as an entrepreneur.

One of his "businesses"?
Renting out an apartment on short-term rental.

And because he couldn't afford a cleaning lady?

Excuses, excuses...

So who cleaned the apartments?

Him.

His friends.
And eventually… **he expected me to do it.**

Yes, really.

One day, while I was still dying from Covid, he **started yelling at me**.

Why?

Because he wanted me to get up, in my near-death state,
and help him clean his **short-term rental**.

…

Can you imagine?

The Grand Escape

At that moment, my **survival instincts** kicked in.

Still exhausted. Still barely breathing.

I packed my suitcase
and dragged myself to the airport.

The next day, I was back in Paris.

Was it over?

Of course not.

A man like this doesn't just let go of a golden treasure like me.

The love messages.
The dramatic begging.
The desperate pleas to return…

And the best part?

I still had personal belongings at his place.

Correction again: **his mother's place**.

Did he return them?

Of course not.

At this point, I just hope my designer coat will one day show up on Vinted.

And you know what?

If it does, I might just buy it back—**out of sheer irony.**

CHAPTER

9

DATING LIKE A PRO (OR AT LEAST SURVIVING IT)

After enduring an impressive number of romantic disasters with French men, I had to ask myself:

> Is dating in France actually romantic…
> Or is that just a well-marketed myth?

Because let me tell you—my experiences did **not** involve whispered poetry along the Seine.

And before anyone says something: **yes**, I live in Paris. I've been here for over a decade. I'm a proud French citizen. Fully integrated.

My best girlfriends are French—and **they're struggling too**.

So clearly, it's not a "foreigner misunderstanding the culture" issue.
It's either a **dating issue**… or just a **men issue**.

As I read recently on social media:

> *"Women have realized it's better to be alone than to feel alone in a relationship."*

After my last attempt at dating?
I couldn't agree more.

Exhibit A: The Man-Child

I once went on a second date with a man who took me to the theatre for a comedy show at 5 PM.

The play ended at 6:30 PM, and I naturally assumed we'd grab a drink or have dinner afterward.

Silly me.

Instead, he turned to me and casually suggested:

> "Let's take the metro to your place."

Excuse me?

Ah, I see how this works.
No dinner. No effort. Just a direct train to the **promised land**.

I smiled sweetly and said,

"Let's have a drink first."

During the drink, I decided to test him.

"Or maybe we will go to your place instead?"

And that's when he dropped the bomb:

"Well, I live with three roommates."

Three. Roommates.

The man was **45**.
Forty-five.

At that moment, I had never been more grateful for my own space.

That night, I walked into my apartment, stretched out on my bed,
and enjoyed my beautiful, peaceful, gloriously roommate-free loneliness
like never before.

The Dating Audit

Following that catastrophe, I had a session with my psychologist.

Together, we did what any logical person would do:

A full-scale **dating autopsy**.

We analyzed every man I had dated, and the results?

Let's just say they were… enlightening.

Men over 40 who are single, never married, no long-term relationship history?

They were rejected by women.
Nobody wanted them.

Men over 40 who are divorced?

Traumatized.
And most of them aren't doing the work to heal.

These men need a minimum of **5 to 7 years** to recover—
if they ever do.

So how does one navigate this minefield?

Simple.

A rigorous **elimination process**.

The First-Date Interrogation

To save time (and sanity), I now arrive at every date armed with
The Questionnaire — created with my psychologist.

Here it is:

- Do you have kids?
- Do you have kids with one or more women?
- Are you married?
- Do you have a girlfriend?
- Is there any woman who thinks she's in a relationship with you?
- Do you live alone?
- Do you rent or own your home?
- Are you stingy with money?
- What was the reason for your breakup or divorce?
- Are you jealous for no reason?
- Where did you go on your last vacation?
- What are your hobbies?
- How do you spend your free time?
- Are your parents alive? Are they sick?

Yes, it's a bit intense.

But so is wasting my time on a **45-year-old with roommates**.

I like to think of it as:

Quality control.

CHAPTER

10

IMPATIENT TRADER

You know that feeling when dating becomes a never-ending disappointment? I took a long break from it. I focused on my business, thrived, and then realized that if I didn't want to die alone surrounded by candles and self-help books, I should probably put dating back on my calendar. I decided: two dates per month. Let's see who passes.

So, as the organized businesswoman I am, I decided to apply the same rules, values, and standards I use in business... to men. I started treating them like leads—potential investments of my time, energy, and future. But this time? No time-wasters allowed.

Selection Checklist: Because My Time Is Precious

Dating in France is a game of patience—men are supposed to write first. No problem. I crafted my profile like a marketing funnel, filtering out the weak ones before they even got to me:

> *"Looking for someone who can match my wit, challenge my mind, and make me laugh. Bonus if you can cook. Casual dating first, taking things slow. P.S. I don't like small talk."*

And now? Let the elimination begin:

Rule #1: If a man's grand romantic opening line is "Hello" or "Bonjour," expecting to impress me with minimal effort—next.

Rule #2: If he proposes a date but magically disappears when I ask for a video call 48 hours before—clearly fearing exposure—next.

Rule #3: If, 48 hours before the date, I don't have a set time and place (so I can check if the venue is actually worth my heels)—next.

> Some even ask, "Where do you want to go?" Honey, if you don't know where we're going, I'm not going. Next.

Rule #4: If we go on a date and when the bill comes, he swipes his company card and asks for proof of payment for his accounting records—next.

> Honey, if you can't afford coffee, you definitely can't afford me.

Rule #5: If the bill is about to hit the table and he suddenly has an urgent biological need to visit the restroom—your wallet stays in your bag. He pays. And then? Next.

Rule #6: If he can't pick a café—pick one that will test his soul.

And then, I matched with *him*.

He sent me a Super Like—attention grabbed. His approach? Intriguing. Our 30-minute pre-date call? Engaging.

Gosh. I liked this guy.

He wasn't French like the others. That was my very first thought.

He was Mediterranean—the kind with perfect espresso, intense eyes. He lived part-time in Paris and was well integrated into Parisian life. So, technically... French. But this important detail? Revealed later.

His charm wore off fast when it became clear it was built on empty plans and borrowed intimacy.

Trader archetype. Super smart. A calculated risk-taker.

He took me to one of my favorite places for a drink. Thirty minutes in—he kissed me. Unexpectedly. Fast. A stolen kiss. And just like that, I fell into my own trap.

You know that feeling when you play the game—dressing sexy, exuding mystery, radiating irresistible energy—knowing nothing will happen? Yeah… it doesn't work with Trader.

He is fast. Impatient. Hot.

And me? Trapped.

How Do You Escape Your Own Trap?

The logical answer? Regain control of the situation.

The problem? Dopamine and pheromones don't care about logic.

This man followed his own rules. Women followed his rules.

And me? I was looking for a way to flip the script.

And I did.

But first—I had to understand where this attraction came from.

The Science of Attraction: Why He Hooked Me Instantly

Something about him felt familiar. Like I had met him before in another life… or at least in another questionable decision.

Attraction, especially the kind that hits you like a train, is a mix of biology, psychology, and energy.

The Chemistry Cocktail: Why Was I So Drawn to Him?

Attraction isn't random—it's a highly potent mix of hormones, energy, and subconscious recognition. A cocktail so intoxicating, it leaves you craving more before you even realize what's happening.

The Subconscious Pull:

The *"Familiar Stranger"* Effect – Sometimes, attraction whispers: *I know you.* Maybe he reminded me of a past lover. A childhood memory. Or worse—a toxic ex I never fully healed from. The subconscious loves patterns, even dangerous ones.

My nervous system screamed: *"I know this place. It feels like home—but not the safe one. Lucia, run!"*

Let's be real. What it truly was, was anxiety.

The Trader wasn't good for my nervous system. And those butterflies in my stomach? That wasn't chemistry. That was cortisol.

This is what emotionally unavailable men do: they wrap charm in chemistry and call it connection.

Attraction isn't just about looks—it's the way someone sees you. The way they speak, how they move, the subtle cues that align perfectly with your subconscious cravings.

And that night? He had it all.

I could already hear the voice of my psychologist screaming in my head:

"Do NOT sleep with him."

Well… this one felt worth the sin.

Interrogation Time: The Trap Question

I had to stay on guard. So, I pulled out my secret weapon:

The List of Psychologist-Approved First-Date Questions.

Because what you don't ask, you don't know. And men? They rarely volunteer the truth.

He passed the initial questions smoothly. Until…

Me: "Is there any woman who might think she's in a relationship with you?"

Him: *Pause.*

Him: "That's a trap question."

Me: "Exactly. And you're trapped."

Game. On.

I looked straight into his eyes, voice steady, certainty radiating.

> "If you want a second date with me, I must be the only one."

No hesitation. No softness. Just raw, unapologetic truth.

> "I'm an all-or-nothing woman. I want exclusivity because I want the full experience. The slow, intoxicating build-up. The teasing. The craving. And when I finally let go—it will be explosive."

I tilted my head, a knowing smile playing on my lips.

> "And you know what? I'm not negotiating. I'm commanding."

Because this need is **unnegotiable**.

He paused. Stared. Analyzed.

Then, with a slow nod, he finally spoke:

> "You will get it."

And just like that—I had him.

Hooked.

The Illusion & The Truth

We had been dating for a few weeks already. The conversations? Brilliant. The humor? Effortless. Time together? Easy, flowing.

And yet—something felt off.

I didn't notice it in my mind at first. I noticed it in my body.

My feminine body—the wise, intuitive compass that never lies—began to shut down.

I couldn't relax around him. I didn't feel soft or safe.

My nervous system whispered before my brain caught up: *Something is wrong.*

It wasn't dramatic. It wasn't loud. But it was **undeniable**.

We were dating for two months. He never once took me to a restaurant. Not because he was simple. Because he was strategic.

Everything was calculated.

Home settings only—low cost, high control. Last-minute plans—so I stayed off balance. No structure, no clarity—just enough attention to keep me orbiting his silence.

He offered intimacy without presence. Seduction without substance.

It wasn't romance. It was emotional manipulation wrapped in glitter.

He wore charm like cologne. Spoke with depth, but lived on the surface.

And for a moment, I called it magnetism.

But my body knew the truth.

Then came **Saturday**. A late lunch. His smile? The same. But the energy? Foreign.

My body shut down. Attraction gone. Warmth gone. Cord—cut.

I knew: he had been with someone else.

He didn't need more women. He needed more mirrors. He hated his own reflection and patched the cracks with attention.

He wasn't seducing because he loved women. He was seducing because he couldn't love himself.

And I? I left.

No accusations. No begging. No closure. Just the kind of silence that haunts a man who's been seen—and will never be touched again.

The Boundary That Broke the Illusion

> "This dynamic doesn't work for me. I'm not available for crumbs."

No shouting. No tears. No manipulation. Just truth. Embodied truth.

And in that instant, I saw something crack—not his mask, not his charm—**his illusion.**

The illusion that I'd stay in limbo. The illusion that breadcrumbs were enough.

My boundary wasn't a wall—it was a **mirror**. It reflected who he truly was. And forced him to feel what he had been avoiding:

> The weight of not rising. The cost of not choosing.

That moment didn't just change the dynamic. It changed me.

I saw the power of a woman in her worth. I saw how truth doesn't need to raise its voice to be heard.

I don't need to control, chase, or convince. I only need to **stand**.

And when I did? I took the man to his core.

So… did the Trader ever step up?

Of course not.

Men like him don't rise—they **recycle**. Same charm. Same excuses. Same IKEA-level emotional depth.

He's probably still out there, coordinating last-minute "plans," recycling lines over a late-night drink at his place, telling another woman he's not a planner—just "in the moment."

That woman hasn't yet realized that a man who can't book a table isn't building a future—he's just furnishing his ego.

As for me?

I left the table.

And took the whole damn **deck** with me.

PART 2

RETURNING TO SELF – THE RISE OF THE SOVEREIGN WOMAN

After the chaos came the quiet. The void. The reckoning.

This is where everything shifted—not because the men changed, but because I did. I began to see the deeper truth beneath the patterns: the rejection wound, the fear of being too much, the compulsion to over-function and prove. And with every layer I released, I stepped closer to her—the sovereign woman within me.

Part Two is the journey of remembrance. Of rebuilding. Of reclaiming the standards, softness, and sacred power we were never meant to lose. It's where heartbreak becomes healing, and magnetism replaces performance.

These pages are for the woman who's done settling—for love, for crumbs, for roles that drain her. This part isn't just about dating. It's about leadership. Business. Nervous system safety. Feminine energy. And radical self-worth.

This is the rise. The homecoming.

Welcome to Part Two.

CHAPTER

11

THE EPIDEMIC OF LOW STANDARDS

Let's talk about the modern-day pandemic no one is addressing:
Women accepting crumbs and calling it a full-course meal.

Symptom #1: The "Independent Woman" Who Pays 50/50

Ah yes, the classic:
"I'm a strong, independent woman, so I'll pay half."
Nonsense.
Sweetheart, being independent doesn't mean financially sponsoring a man who planned the date *knowing* you were coming.

If a man suggests splitting the bill on a first date, do yourself a favor—**split from the table and leave him with the check**.

Symptom #2: Accepting a Date in a Place You Secretly Hate

"Oh, you want to take me to an underground techno club with sticky floors and overpriced beer? Sounds amazing!"

No. It doesn't.

If you don't like the place, **say it**.
If he can't handle that, imagine how he'll react when you express actual opinions in a relationship.

Your time is precious. Your presence is a privilege.
And your dinner location should reflect that.

Symptom #3: "I'll Just Go With the Flow"

Translation:
"I have no standards, and I will tolerate whatever you throw at me."

Women out here are easygoing and chill when what they really mean is:
afraid to say what they want.

Guess what?
Men respect women who have a strong sense of self.

If you don't want to sit on his couch watching Netflix while he texts other women or plays games on his phone—say it.
If you want a proper date—say it.
If he disappears because you dared to have standards?
Good riddance.

Symptom #4: Tolerating Bare Minimum Effort

"He texted me after five days of silence!"

Honey… that's a **notification**, not effort.

If a man is interested, you'll know. He will text you **right after the date**.
If not, he's not interested. This is the rule in France.

If you're confused, he's not.
Stop making excuses for him being "busy"—
Elon Musk is out here running multiple companies and still has time to date.
Your guy just doesn't care enough.

Symptom #5: Staying When It's Clearly Not Working

He's emotionally unavailable? You stay.

He's still active on dating apps after you've slept together? You stay.
He invites you over but never takes you out? You. Stay.

Why?
Because deep down, you think that if you just prove how amazing you are,
he will magically wake up one day and commit.

Let me help you out:
Get up and leave.

Symptom #6: Answering the Dreaded "Why Are You Single?" Question

Ah, the ultimate trap.
He leans in, smirks, and says:
"But why is a woman like you still single?"

And instead of rolling your eyes and ordering another drink,
you take the bait.
You start explaining.
You analyze past relationships.
You try to sound reasonable.

No. Stop right there.

The correct response?
Stand up and leave.

Or—if you're feeling generous:
"Because I don't settle."

Then sip your cocktail like the goddess you are.
Let him process that.

Because let's be real—
When was the last time a man asked himself that question?
Exactly.

Ladies, we are **not** in the business of:

- Begging for bare minimum energy,
- Splitting bills,
- Or tolerating nonsense.

Set the standard.
Make him rise to meet you—or let him fall off.

Because a woman who knows her worth is not just desirable—
She's unforgettable.

And *that* is the energy you want to bring into every interaction.

CHAPTER

12

RELEASING THE WOUND OF REJECTION

I have always been my father's girl.
My earliest memories are of him holding my hand wherever we went. I was always by his side—sitting on his lap during family visits, feeling the warmth of his presence as we walked together.

My father was the first man who ever held my hand.
The first man who made me feel special.

And then, one day, years later, I felt it again—that familiar, heavy ball of anxiety in my stomach.
What is this?
I tuned into myself and named the feeling.
There it was again: that old wound of not feeling enough.
The sting of rejection.

But who was rejecting me?
The Trader?
Or… my father?

As I dug deeper, memories of him resurfaced.
I had tapped into something much deeper than a breakup—
That pure, loving connection with my father.
The safety. The presence.
The feeling of being held and chosen.

Our relationship became complicated when I moved abroad.
He couldn't understand why I left.
His behavior changed.
His once-loving words turned into hurtful comments about my choices.

I didn't understand why he was like this.
I longed for his approval, his acceptance—
yet I knew I couldn't live the life he expected of me.

Looking back, I see it now:
He wasn't rejecting me.
He was hurt.

He felt abandoned.
Disappointed that his only daughter had chosen a life so different from the one he imagined for her.

And so, unknowingly, I began searching for love and approval in other men.

I kept choosing the wrong ones—men who couldn't truly see me or accept me.
It was a subconscious echo of a wound I didn't even know I had.

Something shifted when I launched my business.
My father became supportive.
He told me he was proud of me.
He asked about my clients. About my results.

And suddenly, I understood something I hadn't seen before:
Business is masculine energy.
Earning money is masculine energy.

As I healed my relationship with my father,
my entire reality began to shift.

I became a woman who once again felt his love—
a love that had always been there.
A love that had been hidden under layers of unspoken expectations and unresolved emotions.

The truth?
My father never really rejected me.
He simply expressed his disappointment in a way that felt painful.

But his love had never wavered.

Our very first relationship with a man is with our father.

Whether that relationship was warm and loving or distant and painful,
it shapes the way we see men—and the way we see ourselves.

But here's the most important part:
We don't need our fathers to participate in our healing.

We don't need their validation.
We don't need their apology.
We don't need their permission to free ourselves from the wounds of the past.

We don't even need to forgive them.
Because sometimes, there's nothing to forgive.

When we heal the story within, the external world shifts to match our new frequency.
When we do the inner work, everything else follows.

Healing the father's wound isn't about changing him.
It's about changing how we hold the story.

And once we do, we stop searching for what was missing.
Because suddenly, we realize—
we were never unchosen.
We were never unworthy.
And we never have to prove ourselves to anyone—
ever again.

What If There Was No Father?

Not every woman has the experience of a father holding her hand, making her feel safe, or being the first man to choose her.
Some never had that presence at all.

Maybe he was physically absent.
Emotionally distant.
Or completely unknown.

So what happens then?

The truth is—**whether our father was there or not, he shaped our understanding of love, safety, and worthiness.**
His presence—or absence—created the foundation of what we unconsciously expect from men.

For women who never had a father figure, the wound often runs deeper.
There was no first experience of being cherished by a man.
No early imprint of safety.

Instead, the nervous system learned that love could be inconsistent.
Unreliable.
Or even nonexistent.

And without realizing it, many women go through life chasing a love they never received—

hoping that *a man, any man*, will finally fill that void.

But here's the truth:
You don't need a father to heal.

Healing isn't about waiting for a man—whether it's your father or a romantic partner—to finally validate you.

Healing is about giving *yourself*
the love, the protection, and the approval you never got.

It's about becoming the presence you always needed.
Learning to trust yourself.
Setting your standards.
Knowing you are worthy—
not because a man says so,
but because *you* say so.

Because when a woman heals her father wound,
something profound shifts.

She stops seeking love as proof of her worth—
and starts choosing love that matches her worth.

And that, right there,
is when everything changes.

CHAPTER

13

A Feminine Energy Woman is Magnetic

The biggest mistake women make?
They overshare, overgive, and overperform—all because of one thing:
Fear of rejection.

The fear of being rejected by a man.

So they give too soon, too quickly, thinking it will make him stay.
Instead, it does the opposite—**he pulls away.**

And when that space is created, rather than letting him miss her,
she panics.
She starts texting.
Oversharing.
Overgiving.

And suddenly—she's predictable.

Predictable is unattractive.

Imagine if Chanel's new collection were predictable—
no mystery, no exclusivity.
Would anyone crave it?
Of course not.

And Chanel isn't for everyone.
It has its own standards.
And as a woman, so should you.

Are You Zara or Chanel?

First, you need to be clear on your brand.
Are you Zara—mass-market, easy to access?
Or are you Chanel—rare, refined, and standing in your worth?

And no, this isn't about physical appearance.

Your value lies in your **education**, **career**,
the languages you speak, your life experiences,
the way you express yourself—
and most importantly, your **standards**.

A high-value woman lives by her standards.
She knows what she will never tolerate.
She doesn't shrink herself to accommodate a man—
she raises the bar.

There is nothing more powerful—more sexy—than a woman
who knows when to leave in silence.

And the moment you do that,
the dynamic shifts.

You don't need him to choose you—
because you've already chosen yourself.

A confident woman who knows her worth?
She's **irresistible.**
She's **magnetic.**

Feminine Energy in Life and Business

But here's the thing—
women don't just make this mistake in relationships.

They make it in **business**, too.

The moment they feel like they aren't getting the results they want,
they panic.

They push harder.
Overwork.
Overperform.
Overgive.

Why?

Because they're running on masculine energy.

I hear it all the time from my clients:
"I have to fight the male ego just to be taken seriously."

When I hear that, I know they are operating from survivor energy—
believing they must play by masculine rules to succeed.

But where does that lead?

Fatigue.
Exhaustion.
Self-doubt.
Overperformance.
Loss of joy.
Deep dissatisfaction.

Because **unhealed masculine energy in a feminine body**?
It creates burnout.
It drains radiance.
It makes her **less impactful**, less magnetic, and ironically—less successful.

A woman in her feminine energy doesn't chase.
She attracts.
She inspires.
She influences without force.
She knows her worth.
She sets the standard.

Feminine leadership isn't about fighting the masculine.
It's about leading **differently**.

It's about soft power.
Intuitive decisiveness.
And trusting your energy more than your effort.

And when she does?

Everything—
Love. Success. Opportunities.
comes to her…
effortlessly.

CHAPTER 14

THE DYNAMIC OF MASCULINE ENERGY WOMEN AND PASSIVE MEN

Women often say they want a strong, masculine man.
But here's the real question:

Are you truly a feminine-energy woman?
Or are you a masculine-energy woman trapped in a feminine body?

Masculine-energy women are easy to spot.
They control everything.
They plan, lead, perform—in life *and* in love.
They don't soften. They don't surrender.
They never fully relax.

And over time, this dynamic kills attraction.

Because even the most masculine man loses desire for a woman who never gives him space to lead.
He checks out. The polarity dies. The chemistry fades.
Game over.

When a Woman Feels Safe, She Softens

A woman naturally surrenders when she feels:

- Deep trust,
- Emotional safety,
- And strong masculine leadership.

When those are missing?
She steps up.
She leads.
She hustles.
And eventually?
She burns out.

And an exhausted woman is not only disconnected from her own pleasure—
She becomes deeply unattractive to herself *and* to him.

What Makes a Woman Feel Safe to Be Feminine?

1. Emotional Safety

She can be vulnerable without being judged.
He listens to her emotions without trying to "fix" her.

He's consistent—no hot-and-cold behavior, no confusion.

2. Grounded Masculine Presence

He's confident, calm, and emotionally solid.
He leads decisions without being controlling.
He doesn't seek her validation, but honors her essence.

3. Sexual Polarity

He builds tension slowly.
He initiates with confidence.
He reads her energy—without rushing or needing it.

4. Energetic Balance

When she doesn't have to be "the man," she naturally returns to flow.
When she's constantly planning, fixing, or leading—she loses her ability to surrender.

5. Respect and Admiration

She sees him as capable, honest, and grounded.
She respects how he lives, works, and walks in his values.
Without respect, she loses desire.

What Happens When the Woman Leads?

1. She Becomes Exhausted

She hustles. She plans. She initiates.
She stops receiving—and starts resenting.

2. She Loses Attraction

She sees him as weak, passive, or childlike.
She feels like his mother or manager.
And let's be honest—**who wants to sleep with their employee?**

3. He Checks Out

Masculine men don't fight to lead.
If she takes charge, he lets her.
And if she keeps doing everything, he:

- Gets passive,
- Seeks someone softer,
- Or disappears completely.

4. The Relationship Becomes Sexless

Polarity dies.
Desire fades.
She's tired. He feels emasculated.
No one's turned on.

What Should She Do Instead?

1. Step Back and Receive

Stop planning every detail.
Stop fixing.
Let him take the lead—and observe.

2. State Your Needs—Then Release Control

Say it once.
Example: "I love when you plan things for us."
Then step back. Let him *show up*.

3. Stay Rooted in Feminine Energy

Choose pleasure over pressure.
Feel more. Think less.
Shift from "What needs to be done?"
To: **"How do I want to feel?"**

When you radiate warmth and confidence—he rises.

Why Some Women Can't Let Go

Because of unhealed wounds.

- *Fear of disappointment*: "If I don't control it, it will fall apart."
- *Fear of vulnerability*: "If I open up, he'll hurt me."

- *Fear of losing independence*: "If I relax, I'm weak."
- *Childhood programming*: "My mom did everything. I have to too."

When Do Men Leave Masculine Women?

They don't leave because they don't love you.
They leave because:

- They feel **replaceable**—you don't need them.
- They feel **emasculated**—you lead, so they shrink.
- They feel **unwanted**—you stop respecting them.
- They feel like **failures**—they can't "make you happy."

A Woman's Power Is in Her Femininity

Want a masculine man?

Then stop being the man in the relationship.

You don't need to become small.
You don't need to give up your success or independence.

You need to **return to your essence**:

- Soft power.
- Radiant presence.
- Embodied standards.

When you stand in this energy, a real man will:

- Pursue you,
- Protect you,
- And provide for you—willingly.

How to Hold Polarity With a Masculine Man

Feminine polarity is not a performance.
It's a way of *being*.

If you want a grounded, leading, masculine man—
You must create space for his energy to lead.

That means:

- Speaking your truth, *softly*—not to control, but to be felt.
- Letting him make plans—even if you could do it better.
- Trusting his rhythm—instead of rushing outcomes.
- Receiving his love, his care, his presence—with grace.

Masculine men don't fall for performance.

They don't chase games, manipulation, or fake seduction.

They respond to:

- Warmth.
- Confidence.
- Depth.
- Truth.

When a woman stands in her feminine energy,
She doesn't beg to be chosen.
She *is* the choice.

So if you want a man who holds you, sees you, chooses you…

You must stop choosing half-love.
Stop reaching for crumbs.
Stop investing in potential.

You must become the woman
whose **presence alone is the invitation**.

Because the masculine will only lead
when the feminine finally stops performing.

Polarity isn't about playing roles.
It's about **returning home** to who you truly are—
and letting love rise from that unshakable, magnetic place.

And the right man either rises to meet her… or falls away.

The Power of Walking Away

Too many women accept the unacceptable.

They date a man, become intimate…
and then see him active on dating apps, pretending nothing's happening.

They feel something is off.
They know when his energy shifts.
But they don't speak up.

Why?
Fear of being left.

If a man is keeping his options open, that's his choice.
But you have a choice too.

Instead of falling into his game,
bring it to the table.
No accusations.
No begging.
Just clarity.

And if he values you—if he understands that you'll walk away without drama—
he will fear losing you.
Because men value what they can lose.

CHAPTER

15

PATTERN OF SILENT LOVE – THE PASSIVE MAN AND THE WOMAN WHO FINALLY LET GO

I've met men who were passive in love.

These were men shaped by years spent in relationships with masculine-energy women—relationships that conditioned them to shrink, shut down, and stay silent.
They had grown used to being unseen, undervalued, and unnecessary.
They didn't initiate dates—they responded if I proposed.
They didn't express emotions—they observed quietly from the sidelines.
Supportive, yes. But distant.

Present, yet absent.

Familiar.

They echoed the energy of my father. And it made perfect sense.

My father loved me deeply, but it was my mother who performed the masculine role.
She led. She organized. She carried the weight of the family.
So love, for me, was modeled in silence—presence without expression.
And I internalized that story: love stays quiet, doesn't speak, doesn't show up, but somehow... I must earn it.

But something shifted.

I realized I am no longer that little girl waiting for a quiet man to *finally* choose me.
I am not here to decode silence. I am not here to work for crumbs.
I want love that is expressive. Love that is alive.
Love that moves toward me with clarity and certainty—not passive proximity.

If this silent love story sounds familiar, I invite you to write your own goodbye letter.
Bring the pattern into awareness.
You are not bitter. You are not angry.
You are simply… **done**.

You choose differently now.

Goodbye Letter to the Pattern of Silent Love

Dear Silent Love,

I see you now.
You've been with me for so long—like a quiet echo in every room I entered.
You wore the face of men who stayed, but never truly reached.
You felt like *almost*... but never *fully*.
You stood close, but never claimed me.

You reminded me of a love I once tried to earn as a little girl—
A love I could *feel*, but not *hear*.
A love that taught me to work for attention,
To overgive for scraps of recognition,
To be strong when all I wanted was to soften.

You were never cruel.
You were just... unavailable.

And still, I chased your silence like it might one day become language.
I tried to awaken your heart with mine.
But in doing so, I slowly forgot the sound of my own.

So now, I say thank you.

Thank you for trying to protect me from disappointment.
Thank you for helping me find my voice through the quiet.
Thank you for teaching me what I no longer accept.

But I no longer need you.

I release the men who sit beside me but do not *see* me.
I release the men who say nothing, but expect everything.
I release the roles where I am the light trying to warm a stone.

I am calling in something new.
A love that **speaks**.
A love that **reaches**.
A love that knows what I am and says:
"Yes. You. Absolutely you."

Goodbye, Silent Love.
Thank you for what you showed me.
I'm choosing differently now.

With peace,
Lucia

Once your letter is written, keep it. Burn it. Throw it away.
Do whatever helps you release it.

And then—**read this next part slowly.**

Hand on your heart.
Or on your womb.
Let the words rewire you.

I Release, I Receive

(Read aloud, slowly. This is a reprogramming.)

I release the pattern of silent love—
Love that stands nearby but never speaks.
Love I have to interpret, decode, or chase.

I no longer confuse quiet presence with connection.
I no longer seek to be chosen through patience.
I no longer wait for crumbs when I am the feast.

I release the belief that I must perform to be loved.
I do not need to achieve, impress, or hold it all together to be worthy.
My softness is my power. My being is my gift.

I forgive the little girl who thought love had to be earned.
I see her. I hold her. I whisper to her now:
You are loved even when you rest.
You are safe even when you do nothing.
You are beautiful even when you are quiet.

I release the masculine roles I inherited.
I release the need to lead, organize, and initiate in love.

I no longer chase energy that cannot meet me.
I no longer reach for those who stay neutral.

I let go of [insert his name here].
Not in bitterness, but in truth.
His passivity is not a reflection of my worth.
I now magnetize a man who *rises*—not waits.

I am open to love that speaks.
Love that moves toward me.
Love that plans, initiates, expresses, and holds.

I am worthy of being adored.
I am safe to be pursued.
I am magnetic in my softness.
I am radiant when I receive.

I now stand in my full feminine essence.
I am a woman who is felt, seen, chosen.

I attract a love that does not confuse me—
A love that meets me in clarity, presence, and devotion.

I am done with patterns.
I am done with waiting.
I am done with silent rooms and loud effort.

I now call in love that feels like home—
But only if the home is built with presence.

And so it is.

CHAPTER

16

BECOMING HER, WHO GRANTS ACCESS

After The Trader, I made a declaration to myself:
"I will not grant access to any man who will not lead."

Women who can live by that truth are deeply healed. Their femininity is integrated. Their standards are sacred.
There is no need to chase, explain, seduce, or fix.

A healed woman does not hustle for love.
She simply closes the gates.

No anger.
No noise.
Just stillness—and a quiet, embodied:
"This is no longer aligned."

That is embodiment.
That is royalty.
That is *Her, Who Grants Access.*

She Sets the Standards—For Herself

She does not set the standards *for him.*
She sets them *for herself.*

She sits, watching—
Not with judgment, but with clarity.
Will he rise to meet her?
Will he claim her with the leadership she deserves?

She doesn't beg.
She doesn't bend.
She doesn't shrink.
She doesn't chase.
She doesn't over-explain.
She doesn't create drama to feel seen.

She simply **waits in truth.**

She knows who she is.
She is clear about what she desires.
She is grounded in what she will no longer accept.

And whether he rises—or fades—
She stays centered.

Because this is not about punishment.

It's about **access.**

Access to Her Is a Privilege

She lets him feel the **weight of her standards.**
Not as pressure—but as privilege.

Because **access to her is sacred.**
And not every man gets it.

She knows she is a gift to a man—
A rare, sovereign, magnetic woman.
She doesn't need to shout it. She simply *is.*

And when she stands in that way?
The right man does not hesitate.
He feels her frequency and says,
"I'm ready. I'll rise."

Mantra

(Read aloud with intention. Repeat often.)

I am the one who grants access.
I don't perform—I receive.
I don't chase—I magnetize.
I don't wait—I choose.
I don't fear the loss of what cannot hold me.
I am not available for confusion, passivity, or emotional poverty.

I am available only for clarity, presence, and devotion.
I am a woman who knows her worth.
And from this place—
I am irresistible.

CHAPTER

17

THE LAST ILLUSION

After everything I had lived, after every red flag I had finally stopped painting white, I truly believed I had called him in. And maybe I had.
The one who arrived with calm presence, Mediterranean charm, and words that felt like safety instead of seduction.
A man who didn't just see me — but steadied me.

From the very first date, there was no confusion. He moved with clarity.
He invited me to dinner, messaged me consistently, told me I was his woman.
There was no game. No delay. No French ambiguity.
Just steady masculine presence.

He held the door open. He chose the wine. He asked questions.

He looked into my eyes like he knew what he had found.

And when he sent me that message after our second date —
"I feel you're my woman, as if I've known you for a long time" — something in me softened.
Not because I needed those words. But because, for the first time, they weren't floating above a hollow foundation.
They were matched with action. With follow-through. With boarding passes and plans.

He told me he would take care of me. And he did.
But not in the fantasy-laced way so many men offer care — like it's a performance.
With him, it felt elemental. Practical. Grounded.
He booked the flights. Made the reservations.
There was no checklist. No drama.
Just decisions. Just presence.

And so, I let go.
I surrendered in a way I never had before.
Not because I was in a trance, but because I was finally met with something I could trust.

I let him guide. I allowed myself to receive.
I rested. I bloomed. I laughed.
I lay on his chest and didn't think once about the past.

For a while, I thought… this could be it.

But a Queen doesn't stay in the softness forever.
She watches. She listens. She notices the edges.
And I noticed something. Slowly, subtly, the rhythm shifted.

He returned to his world — the empire, the obligations, the markets, the deals.
And I watched the space between us widen.
Not violently. Not rudely.
Just gradually, like a door left slightly ajar but never fully opened again.

Messages became shorter.
Days became fuller — for him, not for us.
"Morning" in the morning. "Kiss" at night.
He was present — yes. But in fragments.

And I, the woman who had once promised herself never to accept crumbs, began to rationalize the crumbs again.
He's busy. He's stressed. He's successful. He has kids…

But excuses are a woman's way of betraying her own needs — dressed up as compassion.

So I sat with it.
I didn't spiral. I didn't beg. I didn't ask for more.
I simply felt the ache of being with someone… while still feeling alone.

And then one day, the Queen inside me rose.
Not in anger. Not in desperation.
But in clarity.

I sent one voice message.
No drama. No performance. Just the truth.

I told him:
"I love you. I admire you. But I will not stay in a connection where I feel invisible. I feel I don't exist in your world. And I won't compete with your calendar or your kids. I won't shrink into the background of someone else's masterpiece."

And then, I left space.

Because silence — from a woman in her power — speaks louder than any demand.

You see, men like him — high-functioning, high-performing, used to being worshipped for their brilliance — often mistake admiration for love.
They collect praise like assets.
They manage relationships like portfolios.
And they assume that if they keep you close enough, you won't notice how far away they really are.

But I noticed.

Because I have been the woman who waited.
The woman who adapted.

The woman who filled the silence with hopeful stories.

And I made a vow: *never again.*

I didn't want a man to come back with flowers.
I wanted him to come back with presence.

But he didn't.
Not in the way I needed.
Not in the way that said:
"You matter. I make space for you. I choose you."

Instead, he stayed on the edge of availability —
A man who liked being admired, but couldn't handle being fully seen.
A man who offered intimacy in glimpses, but never let me all the way in.
A man who kept his empire intact, but never invited me to be part of the kingdom.

And that's when I understood the truth:
He wasn't a villain.
He was an archetype.

The archetype of the successful businessman who wants a muse, not a mirror.
Who wants devotion, but not depth.
Who wants a beautiful woman by his side — but not one who challenges his pace, his priorities, or his illusion of control.

And I?
I'm not here to decorate someone else's empire.
I'm here to build my own — with a partner who meets me on the throne, not just at the foot of it.

So I let go. Fully. Finally.

He may still whisper good morning.
He may still say he cares.
But I no longer listen for signs.
I no longer read between the lines.

Because when a woman knows her worth, she doesn't need to be reminded she's special.
She needs to be included.
Fully. Clearly. Consistently.

He entered my life like a prophecy.
And exited like a mirror.

A mirror of all the places I still softened my truth in exchange for closeness.

But the chapter is closed.

Maybe he was the one I called in.
Or maybe he was the last illusion I had to release before calling in the man who was never afraid of my fullness.

What matters is this:
I did not lose him.

I reclaimed myself.
Whole. Seen. Crowned.

And I will never again become invisible to stay loved.

Self-Reflection

So many women ask, *how will I know if it's love or illusion?*

Here's what I learned:
If you have to abandon your needs just to stay in the story, it's not love — it's self-erasure.

You can be in love and still lose yourself.
You can be adored and still feel unseen.

But the real healing happens when you realize:
Being loved is never worth disappearing for.

So love as deeply as you dare.
Open as far as your heart will allow.

But never, ever lose yourself in the story.

Because the right love won't cost your wholeness.
It will *cherish* it.
And *amplify* it.

Guidance: When Success Becomes the Excuse

Many women dream of a partner who is ambitious, respected, and successful.
Yet what we often forget is that *success without presence is just another illusion.*

It's tempting to excuse his absence — his lack of initiative, his silence — because *"he's busy with his career."*

But sovereignty demands another truth:
If a man truly values you, he makes space for you.
No schedule, no empire, no excuse will change that.

What women should remember:

- **Success is not enough.**
  A man can have titles, wealth, and power, but if he cannot look into your eyes, take your hand, and choose you with presence, you are not in partnership — you are in an illusion.

- **Bread crumbs are not love.**
  When you start celebrating the rare text, the rushed dinner, the weekend after three weeks of silence — you are lowering your standard. You are teaching your nervous system to survive on crumbs instead of receiving the feast.

- **Sovereignty means pacing yourself.**
  You do not wait endlessly in the cold. You do not bend your joy to fit his absence.
  You stay radiant, magnetic, and alive in your own world — and if he cannot meet you there, you let the door close.

- **The real man is not the busiest man — but the available man.**
  True success is the man who can build his empire and hold you in his arms without making you feel like an interruption.

The Last Illusion is this:

Believing that if you wait long enough, accept little enough, shine bright enough…
He will *one day* turn around and choose you.

But sovereignty whispers another truth:
The man who is truly yours does not make you wait in doubt.
He shows up — consistently, proudly, without excuses.
He is not afraid to include you in his world.
Because for him, *you are part of the empire*, not outside of it.

How to Break Free from Bread Crumbs

The illusion:
He is so successful, so respected, so busy — if I just wait, he will one day have space for me.

The truth:
Success without presence is absence.
A man who values you will make time — no matter how full his life is.

Step 1: Recognize Bread Crumbs

- He rarely initiates contact, and you celebrate it like a big win.
- Your dates are always squeezed into *his* schedule.
- You constantly make excuses: "He's tired, he's busy, he's important."
- You feel anxious more than adored.

Sovereign check:
If crumbs feel like love, your standard is too low.

Step 2: When It Happens

- Pause. Observe. Don't chase.
- Feel what your body is telling you: unease, tightness, waiting.
- Speak your truth softly: *"I value presence, and I need more than occasional moments."*

- Watch how he responds: aligned men adjust. Unavailable men disappear.

Step 3: Reclaim Your Standards

- Remember your worth. You're not a guest in his kingdom.
- Raise the bar. Ask: *Would I want this dynamic in 10 years?*
- Choose sovereignty over scarcity.
- Trust abundance — the right man *will* rise.

The Sovereign Woman's Standard

A man may be busy.
He may be powerful.
He may be successful.
But if he cannot make space for you,
He is not your man.

Because the man who is truly yours doesn't feed you crumbs.
He brings you the feast.

Embodying Wholeness

When you fully embody your wholeness, you align your Higher Self and human self.
You stop chasing. You start attracting.
You stop spiraling. You start choosing.

You move from fear… to feminine magnetism.

You don't *wait* for proof.
You *decide* who you are.
And reality adjusts.

You collapse timelines with a decision.
You raise your standard with a word.

And just like that — the banquet begins forming behind the scenes.

The Body Knows Before the Mind

There was a moment with the Trader when my body shut down.
My skin went cold. My energy drained.
And something inside whispered:
"This is not safe. This is not love."

I stayed longer than I should have.
But my body had already spoken.
It always does.

The feminine doesn't speak through logic.
She speaks through sensation.
Through chills. Tightness. Warmth. Stillness.

Where the Trader created collapse,
My nervous system froze.

And I finally understood:
The body never lies.
It contracts when something is off.
And it sings when soul meets soul.

No fantasy.
No projection.
Just the truth, felt deep in the bones.

CHAPTER

18

SHOULD WE BOYCOTTE FRENCH MEN?

"My dear Lucia, French men should be boycotted."

Those were my engaged-to-an-Italian friend's exact words.
I rolled my eyes… and then realized — she might have a point.

Because let's be honest: the image of the French man is one of the greatest marketing campaigns in history.
The myth of the seductive intellectual with poetic eyes, a scarf, and wine-slicked words.
The supposed kings of romance.
Masters of charm.
The men who make women feel like muses.

But I've lived in Paris for a decade.
I've seen behind the curtain.

And here's what I've experienced:
The fantasy of the French man is not the reality.

What many French men embody isn't masculine leadership.
It's *passive allure.*
They're often cerebral — intelligent, yes — but so deeply in their heads, they forget that love lives in the body.

They seduce through ambiguity.
Draw you in with vague compliments and philosophical flirting…
Only to vanish into indecision and half-effort.

They want to be pursued.
Yes, you read that right.

They admire feminine women deeply… for about three dates.

After that, you're *too much.*
Too radiant. Too embodied. Too real.
A walking reminder of everything they secretly crave — but don't know how to hold.

French men will say they love feminine energy — but only if it doesn't require them to rise in their masculine.
If it stays poetic. Mysterious. Safely undefined.

Because the moment your softness comes with standards —
The moment your presence asks for clarity, effort, and grounded action…
They retreat.

French men admire your feminine — until it asks for their masculine.

But conscious men?
They *crave* your feminine — because they are *rooted* in their masculine.

And the truth is — this isn't about French men, or Italians, or any nationality.
It's about polarity.
It's about the collapse of masculine energy in modern men —
And the longing of embodied women to finally be *met.*

So no,
We don't need to boycott anyone.

But we *must* stop worshipping charm over character.
We must stop mistaking poetic texts for masculine presence.
We must stop shrinking just to stay loved by men who can't love us in our full bloom.

Because you, my love, are not a *muse.*
You are a *Queen.*

And that throne?
It doesn't belong in French fiction.

It belongs in real life —
With the man who is ready to rise and meet you there.

CHAPTER

19

THE LOVER AND THE LEADER – HOW YOUR RELATIONSHIPS SHAPE YOUR SUCCESS

Every woman who walks the path of healing and remembering eventually reaches a pivotal realization: **How I do love is how I do life.**

Let me explain.

If you're choosing emotionally unavailable men, hustling for their affection, proving you are enough...
You're likely doing the same in your business.
Overgiving. Overperforming. Proving your value.
There is no spaciousness. No flow. Only effort.

Love and leadership are not separate.
They're mirrors.

If you accept breadcrumbs in love, you also accept being underpaid or overlooked in business.
If you chase love, you also chase clients.
And worst of all — you believe you must do it all yourself to be worthy of success.

Sound familiar?

Many women I work with come to me thinking they have a business problem: burnout, money blocks, inconsistent clients, lack of visibility.
But after one honest conversation, it's clear —
The real block is polarity.
They're stuck in masculine overdrive — because they don't feel safe to soften.

When a woman leads from wounded masculine energy, she's in control mode.
She doesn't trust.
She micromanages every outcome.
She sacrifices joy for performance.
And eventually? She crashes.

But when she heals the wounds that made her overfunction in the first place — especially in love — something magical happens.
She remembers her feminine essence.
Her softness.
Her magnetism.

And here's the secret no one tells you:

A woman who reclaims her feminine energy in love becomes a powerhouse in business.

Because she no longer hustles.
She no longer proves.
She **attracts**.

She sets standards — in love and in leadership.
She doesn't beg to be chosen — by men or by clients.
She becomes the woman who chooses herself.

The more I stepped into my feminine in love —
The more I allowed men to lead, provide, and pursue
—
The more money I made.
The more aligned clients I attracted.
The more deeply I trusted myself.

My nervous system calmed.
My creativity exploded.
And my business finally reflected the woman I had become.

Because feminine leadership isn't soft — it's sovereign.
It's not about giving up power.
It's about reclaiming it in a new way.

The feminine woman is magnetic, not manipulative.
She's intuitive, not chaotic.
She's clear, not controlling.

And when she meets a masculine-energy man — one who sees her, holds her, and provides for her — her whole world shifts.
She no longer has to lead everywhere.
She can surrender at home and rise in the world.

Your Inner Union Determines What You Attract

When your inner masculine and feminine are in harmony, both your relationships and your business expand.
You stop chasing.
You start receiving.

So if you're reading this and wondering why your business feels hard…
Why clients don't flow…
Why you feel constantly tired…

Ask yourself:

- Where am I still holding the masculine role in love?
- Where do I not feel safe to soften?
- Where am I trying to be chosen instead of choosing myself?

Because once you shift this, **everything else shifts.**

You become the woman who holds polarity in love and in leadership.
You become the woman who is irresistible — in business and in life.
You become the woman who leads not from proving, but from **presence**.

And from there... the world has no choice but to rise to meet you.

For the Woman Who Knows There's More

If you've ever stayed too long...
Waited too quietly...
Loved too loudly... for someone who couldn't meet you —
This book was written for you.

If you've ever abandoned yourself for the hope of being chosen...
If you've ever felt like your softness was a liability...
If you've ever known, deep down, that you were meant for **more** than scraps of attention —
Then this is your invitation:

You're not here to prove you're worthy.
You're here to remember that you always were.

What I discovered through the heartbreaks, the delays, the silence, and the *almosts* is this:

The most magnetic woman is the one who chooses herself fully
— without waiting for permission, apology, or a plan.

And when you become that woman, you stop negotiating for love.
You start attracting it.

If This Book Stirred Something in You...

A remembering.
A reckoning.
A rising.

Then you already know:
Your story isn't over.

Come closer.

I created a masterclass for women like us —
Women who love deeply, lead fiercely, and are ready to stop settling for less.

It's called **Standards That Magnetize™**,
And it begins where this book ends.

Because the woman who raises her standards doesn't just change her love life —
She changes her entire world.

CHAPTER

20

SOVEREIGN WOMAN

For years, I thought sovereignty was something you achieved at the end of a long journey — a shiny badge you earned once you had healed enough, worked hard enough, or proven yourself worthy enough to be crowned.

But the truth is:
Sovereignty isn't given. It's remembered.
And remembering takes time.
Heartbreak.
Voids.
And more than a few French men.

I didn't become a sovereign woman overnight.
I became her through the slow, painful unraveling of who I thought I was supposed to be.

I became her in the quiet moments after breakups — when the apartment felt too empty, and I wondered if I would ever be chosen.
I became her in corporate offices, where I performed excellence like a second skin while my soul quietly suffocated.
I became her in therapy sessions, in hypnotherapy journeys, and on the bathroom floor at 3 a.m. — when the illusion cracked wide open and there was nowhere left to hide.

Leaving my corporate career was my first act of sovereignty.
Walking away from a twenty-year identity that had defined me — the meetings, the titles, the endless proving — meant stepping into a void where no one was handing my validation anymore.

That was terrifying.
But in that void, I started to hear myself again.
My own voice.
Not the voice of my bosses.
Not the voice of my parents.
Not the voice of the men I dated — the ones who always seemed to have an opinion about who I should be.

Healing became the bridge.
Hypnotherapy, NLP, nervous system recalibration — not as tools to fix me, but as keys to unlock the woman I already was beneath the conditioning.

Every heartbreak became less about *him* —
And more about *me*.

What I was willing to tolerate.
Where I was betraying myself.
How much power I had given away in the hope of being chosen.

Because the sovereign woman doesn't negotiate for love.
She doesn't beg to be seen.
She doesn't perform for scraps of attention.

She knows she is the standard.

And here's the paradox:
She's softer than ever.

She doesn't harden to protect herself — because she trusts herself.
She doesn't chase — because she attracts.
She doesn't collapse when life demands more of her — because she leads from a place deeper than performance.

That's what sovereignty feels like in my body: **steady. neutral. unmoved by chaos.**
I no longer wait by the phone for a text that may never come.
I no longer twist myself into palatable shapes so others feel comfortable.
I no longer abandon my own needs just to belong.

And this isn't just my story.
My clients are sovereign women, too.

I've watched women walk out of marriages after ten years because they realized they were no longer willing to shrink.
I've seen executives finally stop people-pleasing in boardrooms and start leading with clarity, grace, and authority.
I've witnessed women who thought they were broken rediscover their magnetism and joy — simply by remembering they were never broken at all.

Because **the sovereign woman doesn't just change her love life.
She changes her entire world.**

And yes — if you'd told me years ago that all the French men — the narcissist, the gambler, the trader, even the "last illusion" — were just training grounds for this…
I would've rolled my eyes.

But now? I see it clearly.

Every heartbreak was an initiation.
Every disappointment was redirection.
Every *almost* was a reminder to stop abandoning myself for breadcrumbs.

**Sovereignty was never about them.
It was always about me.**

And now… it's about you.

Because the sovereign woman is not a myth.
She's not a brand.
She's not just a chapter in a book.

She's a frequency.
One you step into the moment you decide you are no longer available for less than the fullness of yourself.

This chapter is not the end of my story.

It's the beginning of yours.

EPILOGUE

This book was never just about men.
It was never about French charm, red flags, or even heartbreak.

Those were simply **mirrors** —
Each one reflecting the places where I had abandoned myself.
Where I still believed I had to *earn* love, success, or belonging.

But **sovereignty is remembering**.

It's the moment you stop waiting to be chosen and begin choosing yourself.

You don't need to fix yourself.
You don't need to prove yourself.
You don't need to twist yourself into someone else's version of "enough."

You were never broken.

What you needed was to **remember your own standard** —
And to let others rise… or fall away.

A sovereign woman is not louder.
She is **clearer**.
She is not harder.
She is **softer** — because she trusts herself.

She doesn't chase.
She **attracts**.

She doesn't negotiate her worth.
She **embodies** it.

I wrote this book because I know what it feels like to live on breadcrumbs —
In love, in business, in life.

I know what it feels like to wait by the phone, to silence your truth in the boardroom, to believe that if you just worked harder, someone would finally see you.

And I also know what it feels like to stand up one day and say:
Enough.

This isn't just *my* story.
It can be yours, too.

Sovereignty is not the end of the journey.

It is the beginning of living fully.
Of leading with clarity.
Of loving without losing yourself.

You were never meant to shrink.
You were meant to **set the standard**.

The question isn't whether others will rise to meet you.
The question is: will you?

Final Words

Sovereignty is not a crown someone gives you.
It is the moment you remember that you were never meant to beg, perform, or settle.

You were always the **standard**.

And now, it's time to live that way.

For You

For every woman who was told she was *too much*.
For every woman who was told she was *not enough*.
For every woman who waited to be chosen, silenced her truth, or lived on breadcrumbs.

This is your reminder:

You are not here to fit in.
You are here to rise.
You are here to lead.
You are here to love — without losing yourself.

You are, and always have been,
The Sovereign Woman.